MAUNSELL LOCOMOTIVES

JOHN SCOTT-MORGAN

In memory of my mother, Leila Ann Morgan
(17 December 1909 – 24 October 2001),
without whose help and encouragement
none of my life's achievements would have been possible.

First published 2002

ISBN 0 7110 2872 9

Published by Ian Allan Publishing

an imprint of Ian Allan Publishing Ltd, Hersham, Surrey KT12 4RG.
Printed by Ian Allan Printing Ltd, Hersham, Surrey KT12 4RG.

Code: 0210/B1

Introduction

Richard Edward Lloyd Maunsell was probably one of the best locomotive engineers of his generation. His designs for locomotives and rolling stock in Ireland and England were examples of good, no-nonsense engineering practice that won respect and admiration from railwaymen of all grades and positions.

In the present day, many people think of the Southern Railway in terms of Oliver Bulleid and his famous Pacifics (and the rebuilds thereof). However, the impressive array of designs that came from the drawing board of Maunsell's team are, to my mind, of equal note.

Born on 26 May 1868 at Rehemy, Co Dublin, Richard Maunsell came from an old family dating back to Norman times which had eventually settled in Ireland during the 1340s. He attended the Royal School, Armagh, from 1882 and later went on to Trinity College, Dublin, in 1886, to study law at the request of his father. However, young Richard had other plans and had always, from his childhood, had a gift for engineering. He was determined to pursue the engineering interest, regardless of any outside influence or objection, and eventually managed to do this by combining a law course with an engineering course, under the tutelage of H. A. Ivatt, at Inchicore Works, Dublin. Thus by 1888 Maunsell was actively pursuing his studies, with his father being resigned to the fact that his son would follow an engineering (rather than legal) career. At this time it was common for students on a standard BA course not to attend many lectures — as long as they passed their yearly examinations, they could qualify for their final certificate; students were encouraged to attend lectures but not compelled to do so. Thus Maunsell could do his premium apprenticeship and his law degree together.

Left: Richard Edward Lloyd Maunsell, 1868-1945. *John Chaksfield collection*

Right: GS&WR 4-4-0 No 341 *Sir William Goulding*, built 1913. *Ian Allan Library*

Maunsell obtained his BA degree on 1 February 1891, after which he went to England under the Ivatt/Aspinall agreement — an exchange scheme whereby gifted engineering pupils could gain a year's extra training at Inchicore or at the L&YR's Horwich Works, near Bolton.

In March 1893 Maunsell met Edith Pearson, whom he later married (on 15 June 1896) after he had spent a two-year stint on the East India Railway to further his experience and his salary, in order to be allowed to marry her.

In March 1896, at the age of 28, Maunsell became assistant to Robert Coey, Locomotive Superintendent of the Great Southern & Western Railway (GSWR), Ivatt, the former chief, having departed for the Great Northern Railway in England.

Maunsell finally became Locomotive Superintendent of the GSWR on 30 June 1911, following Robert Coey's retirement. Now that he held the top engineering post on the railway, Maunsell wasted no time in producing his first design — a superheated 4-4-0 with Belpaire firebox, which, in truth, had been a final proposal by Coey before he retired. During his time in charge at Inchicore, Maunsell designed two locomotive types — the 4-4-0 (No 341) and an 0-6-0 goods, with inside cylinders (the '257' class), which was underway at the time of his departure to the South Eastern & Chatham Railway (SECR).

In December 1913 Maunsell took up his post as Locomotive, Carriage & Wagon Superintendent of the SECR, after the departure, at 49 years, of Harry Wainwright, who took early retirement. The main task requiring Maunsell's attention was the reorganisation of Ashford Works and the sorting-out of locomotive building and repairs, which had got into something of a mess under Wainwright.

The first locomotive design to receive attention was the 'L'-class 4-4-0, which had, in fact, been the work of Robert Surtees — the man largely responsible for most of the Wainwright locomotives. A set of drawings was despatched to the drawing office at Inchicore for inspection by his former Chief Draughtsman W. Joynt. They duly recommended that the 'L'-class 4-4-0s be given short-travel (instead of long-travel) valves, which affected their performance considerably.

The 'L' class was followed by a succession of rebuilds that helped to modernise the SECR and bring it into the second decade of the 20th century. These included modifying the 'D' and 'E' classes as Classes D1 and E1 respectively, as well as the one-off rebuilding of 'C'-class 0-6-0 No 685, which, after conversion to a saddle tank, became SR No 1685 and remained as a shunter at Bricklayers Arms shed until early-British Railways days. The 'N'-class 2-6-0s were largely the work of Maunsell and Harry Holcroft, who, during his time with the GWR at Swindon, had been involved with the design of Churchward's '43xx' Mogul.

On 1 January 1923 the SECR, together with the LBSCR and the LSWR, became part of the newly formed Southern Railway. The choice of Chief Mechanical Engineer lay between Maunsell and Robert Urie of the LSWR, and, as Urie was of retirement age, it was decided to appoint Maunsell.

There was much to do in order to forge the Southern into a co-ordinated system. Quite apart from the three locomotive fleets involved, there were also three major locomotive workshops and three rolling-stock workshops. Many of the designs inherited from the three former companies needed rebuilding or replacing, and there was the need to design new locomotives and rolling stock. The final orders from the LSWR were a batch of Urie passenger 4-6-0s (later known as Urie 'Arthurs') built at Eastleigh, together with batches of carriage stock from all three railway workshops.

Probably Maunsell's best design was the 'Schools'-class 4-4-0 introduced in 1930 — a small express locomotive which matched the power of a 'King Arthur' 4-6-0 to give great performance. His earlier (1926) 'Lord Nelson' 4-6-0s were impressive-looking but disappointing in their original form (before Oliver Bulleid improved their draughting and front end), and only 16 were built.

In the early 1930s 'N'-class Mogul No 816 was converted for a time to take part in steam heat-conservation trials; this locomotive was later returned to original condition. 'U' class No 629, completed in December 1929, was fitted with a German-design pulverised-fuel unit and operated from Eastbourne shed during the course of this experiment.

In 1928 Maunsell had authorised the purchase of a Sentinel steam railcar that ran on a number of branch lines, before going into store (although not broken up until after British Railways came into being in 1948). He also had a four-wheel Drury petrol railcar purchased, which was similarly evaluated before being sold to Colonel Stephens for use on the Weston, Clevedon & Portishead Railway in Somerset.

The only really dark period of Maunsell's time as CME came during the problems encountered with the 'K'-class ('River') 2-6-4T locomotives in 1927, when there were a number of serious derailments, the worst being at Sevenoaks, which led to their rebuilding as 2-6-0 tender locomotives. It is worth mentioning, however, that the derailments were subsequently attributed more to the state of the permanent way than to Maunsell's design.

In addition to those locomotives constructed for the SR, 26 Moguls, built from parts supplied from Woolwich Arsenal, were acquired by the Midland Great Western Railway and Great Southern & Western Railway in Ireland, where they were known as 'Woolwich Moguls', although none entered service until after amalgamation as the Great Southern Railways. These 5ft 3in gauge locomotives survived in traffic until 1959-62.

In 1925 the Metropolitan Railway acquired parts for the construction of six 'K'-class 2-6-4Ts. To look at these machines one might imagine they were based on the ill-fated 'River' 2-6-4T design, however, they were a tank version of the 'N'-class 2-6-0. The design of which was adapted by George Hally, who, in conjunction with Armstrong Whitworth of Newcastle, modified the Metropolitan-purchased kits. All six became LNER property in 1937, when London Transport handed over operation of the Metropolitan Line north of Rickmansworth. All were withdrawn by 1948.

Maunsell designed a further class of 2-6-4T, the 'W' class, which was used for heavy freight work and cross-London transfer-freight workings. He also constructed the 'Z'-class 0-8-0Ts, which were used for heavy shunting and banking work. These robust tank locomotives lasted until the early 1960s in traffic at Norwood Junction and at Exmouth Junction, from which shed they were used to bank trains from Exeter St Davids to Exeter Central.

SR No A807 in original condition as Class K 2-6-4T *River Axe*, prior to rebuilding as a Class U Mogul in 1928.
Ian Allan Library

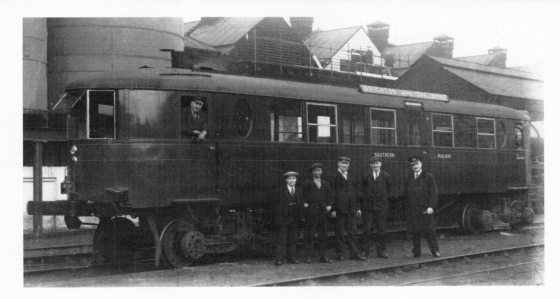

Sentinel steam railcar, introduced by Maunsell in 1928 and used on a number of branch lines, notably that from Brighton to Devil's Dyke.
Ian Allan Library

From the time Maunsell took over the Southern in 1923, he was involved with H. Jones and A. Raworth, the Chief Electrical Engineers, who were responsible for developing the Southern's electric train network. During the time from 1923 until October 1937 Maunsell was involved not only with the electrification of the suburban lines in South and South West London but also with the completion of main-line electric services on the Central Division lines to Brighton, Eastbourne, Seaford, Littlehampton, Bognor and Hastings, from 1933 to 1937. The direct line to Portsmouth was electrified in 1937, together with the outer-suburban services to Guildford, Aldershot and Alton. The new 2-BIL, 4-LAV and 4-COR units used thereon were a follow-on from Maunsell's steam-hauled stock, which had been in production from the mid-1920s and continued into the early 1940s.

Maunsell was also involved in the design and construction of standard freight stock, which continued in production from the 1920s until the late 1940s. During the last months of his tenure of office, Ashford constructed three diesel shunters which became Southern Nos 1-3 and, after fitting-out with equipment by English Electric, entered service at Norwood Junction. In 1940 these locomotives would be loaned to the War Department for use near Dover in positioning the two heavy railway guns, 'Winnie' and 'Pooh', used as part of the Kent Coast defence line.

On 31 October 1937 Maunsell retired as Chief Mechanical Engineer, handing over his responsibilities to Oliver Bulleid. In retirement, he continued to live in the old CME's residence, Northbrooke at Ashford, which he purchased from the Southern Railway, and became involved with the local church which he and Edith had attended for many years. He was made an honorary member of the Institute of Mechanical Engineers in 1938. In his final years, Maunsell would often be called upon to take organised groups around Ashford Works, his last public appearance being on 7 February 1944 at the Dover Harbour centenary celebrations.

Maunsell passed away on 7 March 1944, Edith following just over a year later, on 11 March 1945. Both are buried at Bybrook Cemetery in Ashford. Northbrooke passed to his daughter, Netta, and her husband, Commander Slade. A large quantity of archives was later found in the attic of the house, a selection of which was handed over to the National Railway Museum at York for preservation.

In the years following his death, Maunsell's creations continued to provide valuable service, both in England and in Ireland, the last examples of his steam-locomotive designs not being withdrawn until 1965 (Ireland) and March 1966 (England). His electric rolling stock, in the form of the 2-BIL and 4-COR units, continued in service until the early 1970s. Today a rich legacy of Maunsell steam locomotives and electric rolling stock, as well as passenger and goods stock, survives on many preserved railways and at the National Railway Museum at York — testimony indeed to the talent of a great engineer.

John Scott-Morgan
Woking
July 2002

MAUNSELL IN IRELAND, 1911 – 1913

Left: One of the four classes of locomotive that Maunsell designed for use in Ireland, the 'J4' 0-6-0 goods. In this 1959 picture No 260 is seen with a train of newly delivered steel-bodied stock. The leading bogie carriage is in the short-lived unpainted varnished stainless steel.
Colour-Rail IR579

Below left: Maunsell's last design for Ireland before he left to join the SECR, was this small 0-4-2ST named *Sambo*. This was the only member of its class, being designed as a works shunter at Inchicore Works, Dublin, where it is seen in 1961. It was withdrawn in 1963. *Colour-Rail IR289*

'J4' No 260 again, at Broadstone shed on 6 June 1960. In some respects these locomotives had features that, with modification, developed into the designs later found on the SECR and Southern. *Colour-Rail*

Class L 4-4-0, 1914

The first class normally attributed to Maunsell is the SECR 'L' 4-4-0. In fact, these robust locomotives were the work of Robert Surtees, who was also largely responsible for those nominally designed by Harry Wainwright. The construction of the class was split between Beyer Peacock of Gorton,

Manchester (Nos 760-71), and Borsig of Berlin (772-81), British locomotive builders having full order books in 1914, when the class was introduced. No 31776, built by Borsig in 1914, is seen at Tonbridge shed on 21 September 1958.
Colour-Rail

No 31762 approaches Falmer with a three-carriage local service on 1 March 1959. This was a Beyer Peacock-built locomotive, delivered in 1914. The 'Ls' were originally used on top-link work but had been relegated to secondary duties by the late 1930s. *Colour-Rail*

Left: 'L' in the evening sunlight. No 31775 simmers in the carriage sidings at Faversham on 30 September 1958. There were 22 'Ls', built from 1914. All members of the class had been withdrawn by 1962. *R. C. Riley*

Above: Beyer Peacock-built No 31768 at Eastleigh Works with an LCGB special on 18 September 1960. This beautifully clean example of the class was one of a number transferred from Kent for use on local and parcel trains on the South Western main line around this time. *Colour-Rail*

Class N 2-6-0, 1917

Above: 'N' class No 31871 shunts wagons at North Camp station goods yard in May 1960, while road traffic waits for the crossing to be cleared. The locomotive could do with the attention of a cleaner in this picture. *Colour-Rail BRS1258*

Right: No 31827 heads an up sea cadets' special near St Mary Cray on 18 May 1959. A typical Southern formation, with green Maunsell carriage stock and a utility van next to the locomotive. *R. C. Riley*

'N' No 31811 stands at Stewarts Lane on 30 March 1959, awaiting attention before starting its next duty. Within two years, steam would be largely eliminated from Kent, and a large number of steam locomotives would be withdrawn for scrap. *R. C. Riley*

The last 15 'Ns' were turned out by the SR from 1932 to 1934. No 31405, in ex-works condition at Ashford Works in October 1961, was probably one of the last groups of locomotives overhauled there. This picture shows the locomotive's features well, with a good view of the valve gear and the small fittings, including the AWS box. This is one of the members of the class rebuilt with new front end frames and cylinders by British Railways – clearly identifiable in this view by the outside steam pipe visible behind the smoke deflector. *Roy Hobbs*

In an interesting contrast to the last picture, but again showing the locomotive's fittings in detail, No 31811 is seen inside Eastleigh Works, while undergoing a full heavy overhaul on 6 April 1963.

A rebuilt 'Battle of Britain' Pacific, No 34056 *Croydon* stands behind and a fellow Mogul to its left. The 'N' class was introduced in 1917 and eventually numbered 80 members. *Roy Hobbs*

One of the final batch of 'N' class locomotives which were built with left-hand drive (Nos 1407-14), No 31411 leaves Partridge Green on 22 March 1964 with an RCTS/LCGB special consisting of Bulleid and British Railways Mk 1 stock in BR Southern Region green. The '14xx' series differed from earlier batches in being built with 4,000gal capacity tenders. From 1957 some 47 members of the class carried BR Standard Class 4 chimneys, usually in conjunction with new cylinders or frames. *Hugh Ballantyne*

Class N1 2-6-0, 1922

'N1' No 31876 at Hither Green coaling stage on 5 September 1959. Only six members of this class were built, being introduced in 1922. No 31876 has a straight-sided tender. This picture shows in detail the coaling facility, with its chutes from which coal was decanted from coal wagons into the tenders of locomotives. The steel-framed building was clad in asbestos corrugated sheets — not something that would be permitted today. *Colour-Rail*

'N1' No 31880 makes a spirited start from Bromley South on 6 June 1959 with the 9.35 Victoria–Ramsgate service, comprising carmine-and-cream Mk 1 stock and a single green Maunsell Restriction 1 carriage. *Colour-Rail*

Above: An empty-stock working at St Mary Cray on 16 May 1959, with 'N1' No 31876 heading the train of ex-SR green carriage stock. *R. C. Riley*

Right: Forlorn and rusty, recently stored 'N1' No 31876, in a very different condition from that shown in the last picture, stands against the stock blocks at Tonbridge shed, awaiting its fate on 24 March 1963. None of this class was saved for preservation. *Colour-Rail*

Class E1 4-4-0, 1919

There were 11 'E1' 4-4-0 rebuilds, introduced from 1919 onwards. These locomotives were rebuilt from Class E to produce a machine of greater tractive effort than the existing Wainwright design, to power top-link expresses on the main line from Victoria to Dover and Folkestone. 'E1' No 31507 stands at Stewarts Lane shed on 2 August 1959, while in the background, a Bulleid Light Pacific waits to back down to Victoria for the 'Golden Arrow'. *R. C. Riley*

'E1' No 31067 blows off at Eastleigh shed after hauling the 'North Hampshire Downsman' railtour in May 1960. Note the unusual position of this locomotive's smokebox numberplate. *G. H. Hunt/ Colour-Rail BRS1186*

Class D1 4-4-0, 1921

Above: So successful were the rebuilds of the 'E1' class that Maunsell turned his attention to rebuilding a selection of 'D'-class 4-4-0s, in total eventually numbering 21 rebuilds from 1921 onwards. 'D1' No 31749 stands at Newington station with a train of carmine-and-cream Mk 1 stock on 13 June 1959. *R. C. Riley*

Right: At almost the end of their lives, 'D1' No 31749 and 'E1' No 31067 run light near Bat & Ball station, Sevenoaks, on 4 November 1961. Both classes were withdrawn 1960-2. *R. C. Riley*

Class N15 'King Arthur' 4-6-0, 1923

Left: When Maunsell took over as CME of the newly formed Southern Railway in 1923, a number of designs were on order from Eastleigh for the former LSWR. These included a batch of Urie 4-6-0s, later known as 'King Arthurs'. No 30453 *King Arthur* was one of these locomotives, here seen at Nine Elms in British Railways lined green on 8 September 1958. The disappointing steaming of the Urie locomotives was significantly improved by Maunsell, also fitting his own style of chimney in place of the original stovepipe. *R. C. Riley*

Above: The 30 'Scotch Arthurs' (Nos 763-792) were a Maunsell modification of the earlier Urie 4-6-0s and were built by the North British Locomotive Co in Glasgow from 1925. The balance being constructed at Eastleigh. The 'King Arthur' class, including both Urie and Maunsell examples, eventually numbered 74. No 30782 *Sir Brian* stands in the platform at Oxford with a train bound for the Southern, which includes examples of Gresley and BR Mk 1 stock, on 29 September 1956. A train of ex-GWR Collett stock stands in the centre road, all in carmine-and-cream livery. *R. C. Riley*

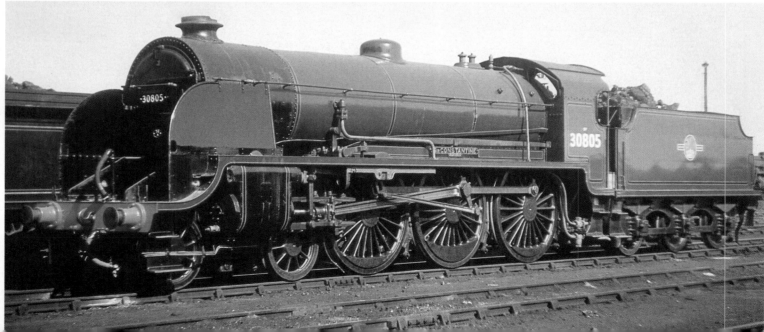

Left: Bathed in afternoon sunshine, two 'Arthurs' in Brunswick green await their next turn of duty at Eastleigh shed in June 1957. On the left is No 30787 *Sir Menadeuke* and on the right No 30784 *Sir Nerovens. B. J. Swain/Colour-Rail BRS395*

Below left: Maunsell 'Arthur' with six-wheel tender: No 30805 *Sir Constantine,* newly overhauled at Eastleigh in July 1957.

A number of 'King Arthurs' were paired with six-wheel tenders, primarily for use in Kent and Sussex, where turntables were smaller. *Colour-Rail BRS560*

Below: A fine portrait of an 'Arthur', again at Eastleigh, showing its gleaming lined-green livery, bogie tender and small BR emblem: No 30791 *Sir Uwaine* in April 1957. *Colour-Rail BRS1082*

Left: The beautiful lines of a great locomotive design: No 30765 *Sir Gareth* at Nine Elms shed on 26 June 1960. This portrait shows the graceful lines of this magnificent machine, with its large driving wheels and high running-plate. *R. C. Riley*

Above: A rare visitor, No 30798 *Sir Hectimere*, at Guildford in June 1962, shortly before withdrawal. The final members of the class were withdrawn during 1962. The only survivor is No 30777 *Sir Lamiel*, preserved as part of the National Collection. *G. H. Hunt/Colour-Rail BRS1261*

Class H15 4-6-0, 1924

Left: The 'H15' was a mixed-traffic 4-6-0 design introduced on the LSWR by Urie in 1920. Maunsell ratified an order for a further 10 placed by the LSWR prior to the Grouping but made no changes to the design, other than to provide the last of the batch with a superheater. No 30524 is seen exiting Bincombe Tunnel with the 13.10 Bournemouth–Melcombe Regis local during July 1959.
G. H. Hunt/Colour-Rail BRS969

Left: Demonstrating the mixed-traffic capability of the 'H15s', No 30521 pounds up to the summit at mile post 31 after the 11-mile climb from Byfleet & New Haw with a lengthy freight bound for Southampton Docks.
Colour-Rail BRS1117

Right: Another view of No 30524, this time at Eastleigh shed on 25 March 1961; along with all other surviving 'H15s', it would be withdrawn later that year. *Colour-Rail*

Class S15 4-6-0, 1927

Above: The development of the 'S15' followed a similar pattern to that of the 'N15' 4-6-0, in that Maunsell developed a design that had been a success during Robert Urie's time on the LSWR. Introduced in 1927, the 'S15s' were often referred to as 'Goods Arthurs' or 'Half-Arthurs' by the locomotive crews, owing to the fact that they were, in effect, 'N15s' with small (5ft 7in) driving wheels, designed to do mixed-traffic work. No 30845 is seen at Yeovil Town shed on 14 July 1962, paired with a flat-sided eight-wheeled bogie tender. These locomotives were always painted plain black in British Railways days. In earlier Southern times, before the war, they had been turned out in full Southern lined green. *Colour-Rail*

Above right: 'S15' No 30839 speeds past Basingstoke shed on 4 August 1962 with a southbound express of Bulleid and Maunsell stock. In the background can be seen some interesting visitors to Basingstoke, in the form of two 'Schools'-class 4-4-0s at the end of their lives and a gleaming ex-works, ex-Great Western 'Hall'. *Colour-Rail*

Right: A sooty and work-stained No 30824 simmers at Feltham shed on 8 March 1964, awaiting its next turn of duty. This locomotive is paired to a Urie-type eight-wheel bogie tender. The 'S15s' lasted in service until the end of 1965. However, No 30837 was stored until March 1966 to work various railtours. *Colour-Rail*

DESIGNS FOR THE SOUTHERN RAILWAY, 1926 – 1938

Class L1 4-4-0, 1926

Left: The 'L1' 4-4-0s were introduced in 1926 for use in Kent on the ex-SECR lines. They were the product of an outstanding order placed by the SECR before Grouping in 1923 to replace old and outmoded 4-4-0s then being withdrawn. Ashford could not accommodate the work, so the order for the 15 locomotives of the class went to the North British Locomotive Co in Glasgow. No 31754, in near-immaculate lined-black livery, stands in the yard at Stewarts Lane shed in the summer of 1958. *W. Potter/Colour-Rail BRS1121*

Left: On 26 August 1961, No 31786 reverses down Woking station sidings during its brief period of duty on the South Western Division. A number of 'L' and 'L1' 4-4-0s were transferred to the South Western area, mostly to work parcels and local stopping services from 1961 to the middle of 1962, at which time all were withdrawn. *Roy Hobbs*

Right: No 31786, in clean lined black, eases around the loop near Tonbridge shed's coaling stage on 11 June 1961. This was the last year of main-line steam in Kent, which finally came to an end only a few weeks after the photograph was taken. *R. C. Riley*

Class LN 'Lord Nelson' 4-6-0, 1926

Left: The 'Lord Nelson' 4-6-0 was introduced in 1926 as a top-link express locomotive, capable of an average speed of 55mph, with a 500-ton train. Sixteen members of the class were built, at Eastleigh Works. This very rare picture shows No 30864 *Sir Martin Frobisher* with a Royal Train at Southampton Docks in July 1948. The locomotive is painted in experimental apple green, lined with red and straw. Note also the Bulleid and Pullman carriage stock. *S. C. Townroe/ Colour-Rail BRS807*

Below left: At Southampton's Ocean Terminal, No 30857 *Lord Howe* waits for the off with a 'Cunarder' boat train for Waterloo in the summer of 1956. Note the mixture of carriage stock — Southern, LMS, British Railways and Pullman — in the formation. *P. B. Whitehouse/Colour-Rail BRS995*

Below: Front-end profile of No 30856 *Lord St Vincent*, showing the cylinder and valve-gear arrangement, at Bournemouth on 23 August 1952. *Colour-Rail*

Left: No 30861 *Lord Anson* at Eastleigh, waiting its turn to work down to Southampton and take the Holland-America boat train to London, c1955. *Colour-Rail BRS1126*

Below: Lord Anson again, this time on shed at Eastleigh, c1955, showing the mighty size of these 4-6-0s. Not as successful as had been hoped, owing to front-end problems, these locomotives were improved by the modifications carried out by Oliver Bulleid in the late 1930s and the fitting of Lemaître multiple-jet blastpipes and new cylinders with 10in-diameter piston valves. *Colour-Rail*

No 30856 *Lord St Vincent* newly outshopped from Eastleigh Works on 18 September 1960 in late-British Railways livery of Brunswick green with orange-and-black lining and 1956-style totem — probably the best-known and most attractive postwar livery. *Colour-Rail*

No 30865 *Lord Hawkins* at Eastleigh in March 1961 in weather-beaten state, still with 1948-style totem, which goes to show that some members of this class retained the earlier BR livery until quite late in life. *D. H. Beecroft / Colour-Rail BRS508*

Class U 2-6-0, 1928

Below: Maunsell further developed the design for the 2-6-0 family by introducing the 'U' class in 1928. These versatile locomotives had larger (6ft) coupled wheels than the 'N' class (which had 5ft 6in driving wheels) and were built at Brighton and Ashford between 1928 and 1931. No 31616 is seen on shunting duties at Redhill in April 1959 in full British Railways 1956-style lined black. Prewar these locomotives had been painted in full Southern lined olive green. *Roy Hobbs*

Right: No 31626 heads a train of Bulleid carriage stock out of Yeovil Junction station on 10 July 1959 while Bulleid Light Pacific No 34041 *Wilton* shunts goods stock in the yard. *R. C. Riley*

48

Left: No 31796 runs through Virginia Water station, heading south with a train of empty Bulleid stock from Ascot in July 1959, presumably from a race special. This line connects the Windsor and Reading lines with the South Western main line at Weybridge via Addlestone. *G. H. Hunt / Colour-Rail BRS1029*

Below: No 31628 awaiting water and coaling at Guildford shed on 11 August 1963. This depot had a large allocation of Maunsell 2-6-0s for working the Reading–Tonbridge line and was, in fact, the last shed to have a sizeable number of these locomotives (up to late 1965). In the background are rebuilt Bulleid Light Pacific No 34001 *Exeter* and 'U'-class 2-6-0 No 31613 on shed in the yard. *Hugh Ballantyne*

Class U1 2-6-0, 1928

Below: The 'U1' 2-6-0s were introduced in 1928 as a three-cylinder design for mixed-traffic work. The class also incorporated the solitary three-cylinder 2-6-4T No A890 *River Frome*, rebuilt as a 2-6-0 tender locomotive in 1928 after the Sevenoaks disaster. As the Holcroft valve gear fitted to the prototype 'N1', No 822, was proving troublesome, Maunsell had Walschaerts valve gear fitted to the 'U1s', except for No 890, which retained the Holcroft valve gear it ran with in its original 2-6-4T form. In September 1957 No 31898 eases out of Southampton Central station with a Brighton–Salisbury service made up of carmine-and-cream Mk 1 stock. The train is framed by the well-known Southampton signal gantry. On the far right a 'T9' 4-4-0 waits in the bay. *B. J. Swain/Colour-Rail BRS414*

Right: At Ramsgate station in June 1959, 'U1' 2-6-0 No 31909 pulls forward with empty stock from a summer special. A proportion of the 21 members of the class were allocated to Kent sheds at this time, working semi-fast trains around Kent and East Sussex. Like the other 2-6-0s, the 'U1s' were painted in lined olive green before the war. *G. H. Hunt/Colour-Rail BRS1032*

Below: No 31891 at Stewarts Lane shed on 6 August 1960. With only a year to go before main-line steam finished in Kent, the 'U1' 2-6-0 waits for its next turn of duty, while a British Railways 'Standard 4' 2-6-4T blows off its safety valves in the road behind. *R. C. Riley*

Right: At Norwood Junction shed on 13 April 1962, shortly before its withdrawal from traffic, 'U1' 2-6-0 No 31906 awaits its next turn of duty, surrounded by other Maunsell 2-6-0s and a British Railways 'Standard 4' 2-6-4T. *R. C. Riley*

Class Z 0-8-0T, 1929

Below: The 'Z'-class 0-8-0Ts were designed for heavy shunting and hump shunting in the Southern Railway's larger marshalling yards. Eight members of the class were built, being distributed at various large yards across the Southern system. No 30953 is pictured here at Exmouth Junction shed on 19 April 1960, while sharing a running road with an Adams 'Radial' 4-4-2T. *Hugh Ballantyne*

Right: Reflections of 'Zs' Nos 30955 and 30952 at work, as the two members of the class climb the bank towards Exeter Central on 3 November 1962, while banking an engineers' train of ballast hoppers, with a 'Shark' brake van. The class was withdrawn from traffic shortly after this picture was taken, being replaced at this location by ex-GWR '57xx' pannier tanks. *Colour-Rail*

Class V 'Schools' 4-4-0, 1930

Left: Following the successful introduction of the modified 'N15' and 'Lord Nelson' 4-6-0s, Maunsell was asked by the Southern Board to consider an idea for a powerful small express locomotive to work on secondary lines, with a capability of hauling loads of up to 400 tons at 55mph. The original idea of a 4-4-0, with as many 'Lord Nelson' parts as possible, had to be abandoned, because the Board insisted that the locomotive should be able to work on the Hastings line, which had a loading gauge restriction of 8ft 6½in enabling the passing of trains in the narrow tunnels on the line. The result was a locomotive combining the round-topped firebox of the final batch of 'King Arthurs' with some 'Lord Nelson' parts. This very rare postwar picture shows No 922 *Marlborough* in full Bulleid malachite green at Dorchester in 1948, only months after nationalisation. The locomotive is in original Maunsell mechanical condition, with small chimney. *S. C. Townroe/Colour-Rail SR35*

Below left: No 30917 *Ardingly*, fitted with a large Bulleid chimney, at Tonbridge shed on 15 April 1958, still in mixed-traffic lined British Railways black livery. Next to it stands an ex-SECR 'birdcage' brake, now in use as an engineers' carriage. *R. C. Riley*

Below: An unidentified 'Schools' 4-4-0 heads an express of Southern Railway Maunsell, Bulleid and British Railways Mk 1 stock along the coast between Dover and Folkestone c1959. The train has just left the Shakespeare Tunnel and is running under Shakespeare Cliff. *Colour-Rail BRS452*

Below: No 30918 *Hurstpierpoint* stands at Willesden shed after bringing a special train across from the Southern to the London Midland Region in July 1960. In the background can be seen one of the Bulleid Co-Co diesels of 1951 and a newly delivered Type 2 Bo-Bo diesel, both in overall green, before the introduction of yellow warning panels. *Colour-Rail BRS322*

Right: In May 1961 'Schools' No 30928 *Stowe* (now owned by the Maunsell Society on the Bluebell Railway) heads a parcels train from Hastings to Ashford at Ham Street station. The locomotive, resplendent in lined green livery, looks very fine, with its original small Maunsell chimney. This locomotive spent many years at the National Motor Museum at Beaulieu and also on the East Somerset Railway at Cranmore, before going to the Bluebell Railway. *D. C. Ovenden/Colour-Rail BRS639*

A time-worn No 30924 *Haileybury* shares a running-road with an 'H'-class 0-4-4T at Ashford shed in June 1961. This locomotive has a Bulleid wide chimney, of a type fitted from the late 1930s onwards, although not all 'Schools' received them; at least a third of the class retained Maunsell chimneys to the end. *A. Sainty collection/ Colour-Rail BRS1036*

Right: Profile of a 'Schools': No 30926 *Repton* in ex-works condition at Ashford shed on a railtour on 25 February 1962, only months before withdrawal and preservation, originally at the Steam Town Foundation, Vermont, USA. Thankfully this locomotive has now returned to Britain, where it is more widely appreciated, and can be seen on the North Yorkshire Moors Railway. *Roy Hobbs*

Class W 2-6-4T, 1931

Following the disaster at Sevenoaks in 1927 which had resulted in the wholesale withdrawal and conversion of all the 'River' 2-6-4Ts to 2-6-0 'U'-class tender locomotives, the Southern Railway did not build any new tank locomotives, apart from the 'Z'-class 0-8-0Ts in 1929. However, there was a need for a class of locomotives to haul heavy freight trains across London and to and from main marshalling yards. To this end it was decided to build a new tank class using parts stored from the 'River'-class 2-6-4Ts and using the three-cylinder 'N1' class as a basis for the design. Thus emerged the 'W'-class 2-6-4T, largely as a tank version of the 'N1'-class 2-6-0, with improved riding and suspension. In March 1960 No 31924 stands at the coaling stage at Hither Green awaiting coaling-up, immaculate in black with 1949 totem. *T. B. Owen/Colour-Rail BRS847*

A work-stained No 31912 stands at Wimbledon down goods sidings on 25 July 1964. This picture conveys the considerable bulk of this handsome design of tank locomotive. *Hugh Ballantyne*

Class Q 0-6-0, 1938

The 'Q'-class 0-6-0 was the last steam locomotive designed by the Maunsell team before he retired. Only 20 were built, primarily to replace worn-out Victorian locomotives. There were plans for a Maunsell 'Q1' class (a modified 'Q'), but Oliver Bulleid threw out these plans when he took over as CME, introducing his own version in 1941. No 30548 ambles through West Moors station on a sunny day in July 1959, with a pick-up goods consisting mostly of closed goods and parcels vans. *G. H. Hunt/Colour-Rail BRS1019*

On a number of occasions there were efforts to improve the draughting of the 'Q'-class 0-6-0s. In 1955 British Railways made a further attempt which resulted in a single blastpipe of modified dimensions. This locomotive, No 30549, was previously fitted with a Bulleid multiple-jet blastpipe. It is seen at Norwood shed in July 1955, surrounded by 0-6-0 goods locomotives of Class C2X — a type the 'Q' was intended to replace. *R. C. Riley*

No 30546 at Three Bridges shed in March 1963. This is a good profile picture, showing the Bulleid large chimney (an earlier attempt at improving draughting) and the slab-sided six-wheel tender — all in all a rather neat-looking locomotive, not unlike a Midland '4F' 0-6-0 in outward appearance. *Roy Hobbs*

Towards the end of its life No 30543, fitted with British Railways standard chimney, stands at Redhill shed, with a snowplough attached to its front end, in February 1964. The last members of the class were withdrawn in 1965, one, No 30541, going to the Woodham Bros scrapyard at Barry, South Wales, from where it was saved for preservation on the Bluebell Railway in East Sussex. *Roy Hobbs*

REBUILDS, 1923 – 1938

Left: Following electrification of the main lines to Brighton and Eastbourne in 1933 and 1934, the large Brighton Baltic (4-6-4) tanks became surplus to requirements. As they were not suitable for use on any other part of the Southern system, from 1934 Maunsell had them rebuilt as 4-6-0 tender locomotives, reclassifying them as 'N15X'. Still in Bulleid malachite green, No 32333 nears Bramshott Halt with a mixed freight in November 1951. Named *Remembrance*, this locomotive had been the LBSCR's memorial to employees lost in World War 1. *T. B. Owen/Colour-Rail BRS513*

Left: The 'T14s' were probably the best 4-6-0s (of a poor lot) designed by Dugald Drummond for the LSWR. The class was rebuilt twice and had other modifications carried out from just after World War 1 until the late 1940s, in an attempt to improve the performance of these mediocre (at best) locomotives. Awaiting recall to traffic, No 443 stands on a storage road at Nine Elms shed in London in June 1949, with its chimney sacked up and a Maunsell Mogul behind for company. By this time, the class had lost the paddle-box splashers and had gained Urie-style stovepipe chimneys. *T. B. Owen/Colour-Rail SR40*

Seen at Plymouth Friary shed in September 1956, in company with 'B4' 0-4-0T No 30088, is 'E1R' 0-6-2T No 32095, one of 10 former LBSCR 'E1' 0-6-0Ts rebuilt as 0-6-2T in 1927/8 for use on the North Devon & Cornwall Junction line. All survived until the late 1950s, when they were replaced with ex-LMS Ivatt 2-6-2Ts.
J. Harrison/ Colour-Rail BRS967

LOCOMOTIVES BUILT FROM WOOLWICH PARTS

A number of companies purchased parts from Woolwich Arsenal in the early 1920s, among them the Midland Great Western Railway and Great Southern & Western Railway, although none entered service until after amalgamation as the Great Southern Railways. A total of 27 sets of parts were supplied, from which 26 locomotives were erected, the final 'set' being used as spares. Twenty were practically 'N' class look alikes, Nos 372-91, with the final six (Nos 393-398, Class 393 / K1a) having 6ft driving wheels in place of the standard 5ft 6in (Class 372 / K1). Erected at Inchicore Works from Woolwich Arsenal parts in 1930 was No 396, it is seen at Broadstone May 1950. The last member of the two classes of 'Woolwich Moguls' was withdrawn in 1962. *W. H. G. Boot/ Colour-Rail IR288*

The Metropolitan Railway in London also purchased parts to build a class of six 2-6-4Ts. These 'K'-class locomotives were intended for goods work but often worked passenger trains from Finchley Road to Aylesbury and Verney Junction. No 112 is seen still in full London Transport maroon livery on a freight at Amersham in June 1938, shortly after the larger Metropolitan tanks were handed over to the LNER. They were built by Armstrong Whitworth & Co of Newcastle in 1925 to a design by George Hally. *Colour-Rail LT138*

Left: Towards the end of Maunsell's career as CME, he and his team produced three 0-6-0 diesel-electric shunting locomotives, numbered 1-3. These machines had a Southern Railway-built superstructure, while the mechanical and electrical equipment was supplied by English Electric of Preston. Outshopped in 1937, locomotive No 2 is pictured at Norwood Junction in May 1939, in company with 'E3' 0-6-2T No 2167 and an 'E6' 0-6-2T waiting for the road. A train of electric suburban stock can be seen in the background.
C. S. Perrier collection/ Colour-Rail SR56

Left: Although loaned to the War Department between 1941 and 1945, they were returned to the Southern Railway and became British Railways property in 1948. No 15201 is seen at Eastleigh shed in November 1963. *M. Burnett/ Colour-Rail DE927*

Another view of No 15201 at Eastleigh shed c1961, still in early BR black livery but sporting wasp-stripe bonnet markings. At this time No 15202 was at Ashford, while No 15203 was at Norwood Junction. All three were withdrawn for scrap in 1964.
L. E. Elsey/Colour-Rail DE1941

Left: Along with the Southern Railway's electrical engineers, Maunsell was heavily involved with the design of electric rolling-stock, from 1923 until his retirement in 1937. 4-LAV unit 2922 runs through South Croydon on a down Brighton semi-fast in August 1967. The first unit of this stock emerged from Eastleigh Carriage Works in the summer of 1931, for use on the newly electrified Brighton and Eastbourne main lines, the 4-LAV classification indicating a four-car, lavatory-equipped unit. Further units were built at Eastleigh up until 1940. The last two resembled 2-HAL units in body design. *A. M. Logan/Colour-Rail DE1622*

Above: 4-LAV in a panorama at Brighton station on 30 May 1964, showing the famous overall roof of the station (now listed) and in the background the former Works offices. The 4-LAV stock was gradually withdrawn during 1969. None was painted British Railways blue. *Colour-Rail*

In 1932 the Southern Railway introduced 20 six-car main-line units, each with a single Pullman car. These units, classified as 6-PUL and 6-CITY, ran between London Victoria and Brighton and also Victoria and West Worthing. This is unit 3041 with Pullman car *Gwladys* (third car in), on 16 May 1966. The majority of this stock was withdrawn for scrap in 1966. *Colour-Rail*

Right: Pullman panorama on 19 March 1967, as 5-BEL set 3052 leaves Victoria *en route* to Brighton. The 'Brighton Belle' was the world's first all-Pullman electric train and ran between London Victoria and Brighton from 1933 to 30 April 1972, having replaced the earlier steam-hauled 'Southern Belle', which dated back to LBSCR days. *Colour-Rail*

Below right: 5-BEL unit 3052 speeds through Wandsworth Common *c*1963, in full Pullman chocolate and cream. These units were later repainted in British Railways blue and grey, which never really suited them. After withdrawal in 1972, most of the cars were sold for preservation, but, alas, none was kept for the National Collection, which had a bias towards steam locomotives. *Colour-Rail DE843*

Left: The first batch of 2-BIL units entered service on the Eastbourne line in early 1935. Used for semi-fast services on Southern electric lines along the coast from Hastings to Worthing and Littlehampton, they also operated stopping trains on the Brighton and Eastbourne main lines. Unit 2003, however, is seen near Liss on a Waterloo–Portsmouth working on 27 January 1968, still in green livery, with small yellow panel. *Colour-Rail*

Below left: 2-BIL unit 2114 at Waterloo in August 1970, not long before its demise. From 1968 a sizeable proportion of the BIL stock was repainted in British Railways blue, and some of the last survivors were operated on the Waterloo–Reading services in the early 1970s. One, preserved as part of the National Collection, is currently in the custodianship of the Suburban Electric Railway Association in Hastings. *Colour-Rail*

Right: The 4-COR units were introduced in 1937, for use on the newly electrified Portsmouth direct line via Woking and Guildford. They were, however, also used on the Victoria–Portsmouth Harbour services via Horsham. Unit 3107 runs through Petersfield station with a Portsmouth Harbour–Waterloo service in September 1969. After displacement from main line work, these units were used on secondary services along the coast and also on Waterloo–Reading services until September 1972. From 1968 they were painted British Railways blue. One complete four-car unit is preserved by the Southern Electric Group at St Leonards-on-Sea, and an additional motor driving car is preserved in the National Collection at York. *Colour-Rail*

Right: The 2-HAL stock was introduced in 1939, after Maunsell's retirement. These units were intended for use on the London–Maidstone/ Gillingham electrification, but, owing to their early delivery, were used initially on a number of other routes. Unit 2632 stands in the platform of Three Bridges station in August 1955, resplendent in overall green. All were withdrawn by 1971. *Colour-Rail*

Acknowledgements

I should like to thank the following people for their kindness in loaning me material, not least the numerous colour transparencies, during the production of this volume: Messrs R. C. Riley, Roy Hobbs, Hugh Ballantyne, and Ron White of Colour-Rail. If I have driven any of the above mad by my frequent requests for more material, I am very sorry — I was only trying to cover as much as possible in a small amount of space. I also made reference to the following volumes for detailed information:

Maunsell Locomotives, B. Haresnape
   (Ian Allan Publishing);
*Southern Electric Multiple-Units
   1898 – 1948*, Colin Marsden
   (Ian Allan Publishing);
Locomotives of the Southern Railway,
   D. Bradley (RCTS);
The Great Southern & Western Railway,
   K. A. Murray and D. B. McNeill (IRRS);
South Eastern & Chatham Railway,
   D. Bradley (RCTS);
*Richard Maunsell — An Engineering
   Biography*, J. Chacksfield
   (Oakwood Press);
The Maunsell Moguls, P. Rowledge
   (Oakwood Press).

Finally, I should like to thank Claire Turnbull, my niece, for putting the text on disk so that it could be published.